I0491018

BECOMING A
PROJECT MANAGER

LOTS OF INSIGHT AS
YOU CONSIDER A NEW CAREER

Addie Adelekan, Ph.D

Archway Publishing books may be ordered through booksellers or by contacting:

Archway Publishing
1663 Liberty Drive
Bloomington, IN 47403
www.archwaypublishing.com
844-669-3957

ISBN: 978-1-6657-1482-2 (sc)
ISBN: 978-1-6657-1483-9 (e)

Library of Congress Control Number: 2021922589

Print information available on the last page.

Archway Publishing rev. date: 11/11/2021

Project management, as a career choice, has been exceptionality good to me. It is exactly for this reason that I chose to write this book, share my insight and progression, and hopefully inspire others to follow a similar path.

This book is therefore dedicated to everyone who is still unsure about what to do with their careers and those who are slightly interested in or aspiring to be project managers. May the profession be as good to you as it has been to me and mine. Best wishes!

CONTENTS

INTRODUCTION

Pursuing a career in project management has been one of the best life decisions that I've made, and I know it is the same for many of my friends and colleagues in the field. For years, as I have looked at every area of my life from family and friends to hobbies and the legacy I will leave, I keep seeing how this career choice has positively impacted the things that matter most. From my first year in this career and even until now in my seventeenth year in the field, I continue to ponder how lucky and accomplished I have felt executing projects and hiring, training, and mentoring project managers.

More and more today, I have met both older and younger people seeking advice about pursuing project management as a career or finding best practices in project management. The purpose of this book is to share some of this information more broadly. In this book, I discuss effective steps for making a career in project management, and I share my career as an example with lessons learned and the various benefits and opportunities for people interested in project management.

My hope is that this book and the supporting resources serve as helpful tools for people who still are not sure what to do, those who are looking to start a fulfilling and fun career in project management, as well as those looking to further take advantage of the benefits and opportunities in project management. Ultimately, my hope is that a career in project management serves many more people across the globe as well as it has served me and those in my circle over the last seventeen years.

UNDERSTANDING PROJECT MANAGEMENT

PROJECT MANAGEMENT IS a seemingly simple concept and popular job opportunity, yet many today do not really understand what project management means. The concept is rooted in two simple words that have been clearly defined over time. The first of these is the word *project*; the second is *management*. The word *project* according to the Association of Project Management describes "a unique, transient endeavor, undertaken to achieve planned objectives, which could be defined in terms of outputs, outcomes, or benefits" (Dixon 2000). And the Oxford English Dictionary describes it as "an individual or collaborative enterprise that is carefully planned and designed to achieve a particular aim" (Dictionary 1989). It is essentially any temporary effort undertaken to meet a predefined goal, and it is assumed that projects generally have the following characteristics (Merry 2000):

- **Projects have a purpose**. Projects have clearly defined aims and set out to produce clearly defined results. Their purpose is to solve a problem, and this involves analyzing needs beforehand. Suggesting one or more solutions aims at lasting social change.

- **Projects are realistic**. Their aims must be achievable, and this means taking into account both requirements and the financial and human resources available.

- **Projects are limited in time and space**. They have a beginning and an end and are implemented in a specific place and context.

- **Projects are complex**. Projects call on various planning and implementation skills and involve various partners and players.

- **Projects are collective**. Projects are the product of collective endeavor. They are run by teams, involve various partners, and cater to the needs of others.

- **Projects are unique**. All projects stem from new ideas. They provide a specific response to a need (problem) in a specific context. They are innovative.

- **Projects are an adventure**. Every project is different and groundbreaking. They always involve some uncertainty and risk.

- **Projects can be assessed**. Projects are planned and broken down into measurable aims, which must be open to evaluation.

- **Projects are made up of stages**. Projects have distinct, identifiable stages.

The second part is not as simple. Management, like many similar phenomena, has as many different definitions as there are theorists and business experts. To understand project management, it can be described as "the art of getting things done through people" (Jones 2013) or "the transformation of resources into utility" (Malik 2015). Its earliest theorists have suggested it includes or is made up of activities like forecasting, planning, organizing, commanding, coordinating, and controlling (Fayol 1916), and in practice today, those are key tasks that most managers remain responsible for.

With these definitions in mind, project management is the practice of working with resources to forecast, plan, organize, command, coordinate, and control a temporary effort. It often includes initiating, planning, executing, controlling, and closing an effort once a predefined goal is articulated. The international governing body for project management is called the Project Management Institute (PMI), and they generally regulate the field. This body describes project management as "the application of knowledge, skills, tools, and techniques to project activities to meet project objectives" (Guide 2004). In practice, project management is done by project managers or others who may be performing as such even without holding the "project manager" title.

The international certificate held by most project managers is called the Project Management Professional (PMP). This certificate is offered through the PMI and can be acquired by passing a test after being approved by the PMI.

Another thing to note is that there are many different types of project managers covering various fields of work. There are business project managers, technology project managers, construction project managers, marketing project managers, and so many others depending on the field of work. Project managers are sometimes very technical in skill set, and other times, they are not. They can be found in virtually every industry doing relatively the same type of work. For example, project managers in construction are usually responsible for managing building projects like homes or bridges. In financial services, the project managers may be responsible for setting up financial systems or working on new compensation or actuarial models. In information technology, the project managers help implement new technology systems like software or hardware systems, or they assist with things like data center upgrades or migrations. In government, project managers help will rolling out new government initiatives like loan programs and/or health-care programs. And in the medical field, project managers could lead the rollout of new services like telemedicine, for instance. Regardless of the industry or type of project management, these individuals are typically leading an effort to deliver on a new initiative that will add value to an organization.

MY CAREER AS A PROJECT MANAGER

MY CAREER IN project management really began while I was an undergraduate student during my internship with the International Child Art Foundation (ICAF). In this role, I worked with a program manager and was responsible for helping to deliver two projects: the International Child Art Festival and the *Child Art* magazine. For both, I worked with others to plan and fully implement the projects. We detailed our requirements and work packages, assigned tasks, encouraged and enabled progress, and held status meetings from the beginning until all the work was done. It was very fulfilling when the magazine was ready with the first project and at the end of the festival with the second project.

Following this, I increasingly leveraged my learning experiences and education on future projects including the following fifty-plus projects:

1. Implementing a go-forward telephone model, including migrating telephone applications and architecture. (Affected applications include Nice Call Recording, Speech and Desktop Analytics, Mattersight, Castel, Aspect Dialer, Avaya, and Cisco UCCE at Wells Fargo.)

2. Managing a portfolio of over twenty different ERP software implementation projects and upgrades at large nonprofit organizations, including Safe Horizon, American Psychological Association (APA), AGRA, and others.

3. Leading the development and implementation training programs for employees and clients.

4. Developing, managing, and initiating a business resiliency plan for IT development and production support teams, ensuring that if the staff, facilities, or technologies are unavailable, the risk is quantified, and the department is able to recover within stated objectives.

5. Designing, developing, and coordinating the implementation of a new organizational structure that optimized the delivery of technology services by a seventy-person team.

6. Managing the production and distribution of a daily IT production support and development report, which helped executive leadership to manage the department's ability to meet service level agreements and reduce operational incidents within the organization.

7. Managing the production and distribution of a monthly business review packet, which serves as a tool for IT leadership to discuss their monthly performance with their business partners (comparison of plans to actual in finance, staffing, and production support, for example).

8. Developing and implementing departmental and project SharePoint sites to facilitate collaboration and document retention.

9. Developing and implementing a resource management toolkit that eliminates confusion and creates efficiencies in hiring employees across a major IT department.

10. Leading the onboarding process for new full-time employees, contractors, and consultants.

11. Coordinating the process to execute new and revised statements of work with consulting vendors.

12. Leading an effort to determine, document, and track performance against service levels for internal and external partners.

13. Leading the rebranding of all Wachovia Securities Financial Advisor field offices across the United States following the merger of Wachovia and Wells Fargo.

14. Developing procedure documents and managing on-time execution of a firm-wide strategic planning process that involved several different business areas and support teams.

15. Designing a process for identifying and rebranding marketing materials for financial advisors after a merger.

16. Leading a mass change of internal and external signs for more than four hundred financial advisor office locations throughout the United States, ensuring brand adherence.

17. Staffing, training, and providing telephone support to over nine hundred field support staff that assisted with a technology conversion project in financial advisor offices. Conversion support staff received special compensation for leaving their homes to temporarily work for one- to three-week durations in offices near and far from their home base.

18. Working with web hosting vendor and internet teams and successfully rebranding more than one hundred financial advisor websites in support of a merger of two large financial services companies.

19. Designing, developing, and administering an enterprise-wide training program for all project managers and business analysts at Lincoln Financial Group.

20. Documenting procedures and other materials while assisting with the IT planning/prioritization processes.

21. Building out a project management center of excellence, including developing a project management methodology and templates, marketing project management support services, and organizing formalized training, lunch and learns, and more.

22. Developing and executing an improved talent acquisition and onboarding strategy, which increased diversity and branded the firm locally as an employer of choice and improved the manager and new hire onboarding process for home office and field support staff.

23. Managing firm-wide diversity initiatives while developing and leading departmental diversity-building efforts.

24. Recruiting top producing financial planners using referrals, internet, industry relationships, and various marketing campaigns.

25. Implementing a national recruit management system for financial planners using existing CRM technology.

26. Recruiting high-potential college graduates into a management training program through college recruiting interviews and presentations.

27. Developing unique strategies for filling open exempt and nonexempt positions in different markets simultaneously.

28. Developing relationships with sourcing agencies, schools, universities, user groups, and minority agencies with the goal of attracting top talent.

29. Managing over one hundred open jobs, including developing the description, posting the job, reviewing applications, interviewing, testing, making offers, and running background checks for several different teams.

30. Planning and executing department-specific job fairs to support high-volume recruiting in several call centers.

31. Implementing a national attendance tracking system to track financial advisor training in field/satellite offices throughout the United States.

32. In support of one of the CEO's priority projects for the year, designing and implementing a major business unit dashboard that contained key metrics like sales, expense, and staffing to support executive decision-making.

33. Consolidating financial reports and reducing redundancy and discrepancies within a large business unit.

34. Designing and implementing an all-employee survey to determine the user satisfaction levels on a web-based human resource tool.

35. Creating sales referral leverage packets for several financial planners using strategic research tools like Lexis-Nexis.

36. Designing and implementing web-based surveys to support project management department goals.

37. Working with an internet team to integrate agency websites and other applications acquired from a merger of two Fortune 500 financial services companies.

38. Implementing post-conversion internet connectivity for an admin system conversion program that consolidated fourteen admin systems into two. Affected admin systems include CLOCS, Life-Comm, Life-70, Vantage, and Term-Paid.

39. Improving an organization's ability to speedily grow internet user groups by decoupling configuration files from a tightly coupled application build process.

40. Working with United States- and United Kingdom-based teams to provide a web functionality that enables United Kingdom-based independent financial advisors to access United Kingdom-hosted systems through a United States-based secure authentication environment in support of a new United Kingdom product launch.

41. Temporarily redirecting agents from one domain to another while integrating several website access points through a single sign-on process in support of a merger in the financial services industry.

42. Conducting a post-merger analysis and go-forward recommendation for the internet environment to support CIO-level decisions and a Fortune 500 financial services company.

43. Redesigning and managing corporate consumer websites and other internet, intranet, and extranet sites.

44. Leading efforts to raise the consumer website industry rankings (Dalbar) to fourth position from thirteenth among life and annuity industry consumer websites in three quarters; website has sustained top four to date.

45. Designing and implementing a secure website for the board of directors of a financial services company in an effort to provide better information access to board members throughout the year.

46. Designing and implementing a website for recent college graduates, their management, and potential hires in a management training program under extremely tight deadlines.

47. Designing and implementing a web-enabled worksite that facilitated team-based collaboration and improved

project management efficiency on document–intensive projects.

48. Developing and managing several division-wide SharePoint sites to allow collaboration and knowledge sharing.

49. Designing and implementing a direct mail and email marketing campaign, which produced great recruiting leads for a national brokerage firm.

50. Designing and implementing internal corporate magazine/newsletter for young professionals and managers who were part of a leadership development program.

51. Auditing the automated interest crediting process, training actuarial process testers to comply with Sarbanes Oxley testing requirements, supervising the testing, coordinating testing resources, and ensuring that all regulatory deadlines were met.

52. Leading the effort to purchase training services from a professional training vendor.

53. Leading the effort to purchase financial calculators for a large Fortune 500 company from a web services vendor.

With all of these, I was directly responsible for project kickoffs, planning, monitoring, change management, testing, deployment, and closing. In some, I was involved with mentoring and training new project managers. Depending on the organization,

I sometimes was involved with defining and implementing project management practices and processes; improving customer retention through various account management practices; rescuing or improving several large, troubled implementations; developing and reviewing proposals, statements of work, change orders, and other business documents; and leading financial matters for my projects or the departments, including budget development and justification, monthly reforecasts, accruals, reporting, and variance analysis.

What was great about it all, in addition to the fulfillment from delivering the projects, was when peers, managers, and other stakeholders began viewing me as an outstanding project manager with significant experience leading both business and information technology projects. I was considered as someone who had strong experience in planning and execution using various methodologies as well as a unique ability to manage several different work streams at different levels of the organization. These perspectives also led to reviews and recommendations like the following:

1. "Aderonke has many areas of expertise, great communication skills, and a positive can-do attitude that would make her a tremendous asset to any company or team."

   • A Project Leader, Lincoln Financial Group

   • Worked directly with Aderonke at Lincoln Financial Group

2. "Aderonke is a pleasure to work with. She is very detail-orientated and customer-focused. While working on projects, she always makes sure that the end goals are strategically aligned with the company objectives. I highly recommend working with Aderonke."

   • A Business Development Manager, ESI International

   • A consultant or contractor to Aderonke at Lincoln Financial Group

3. "I have personally worked with Ade on teams as well as observed her work in a shared office environment. She is a great team player, she is brilliant, she has the highest possible work ethic, and I am delighted to give Ade the best recommendation possible to anyone lucky enough to have her on board in their organization."

   • A National Resource for Advisor Staff Development, Lincoln Financial Network

   • Worked with Aderonke at Lincoln Financial Advisors

4. "I worked with Aderonke on several projects over a three-year period and was always impressed with her professionalism, attention to detail, focus on results, and positive outlook. If I were asked to recommend a team of high performers, Aderonke would be at the top of my list."

   • An Executive Project Coordinator, Lincoln Financial Advisors

- Worked with Aderonke at Lincoln Financial Advisors

5. "Aderonke is a master organizer with an incredible amount of energy. She is very bright, positive, and upbeat and seeks to bring people together in a project environment. I hope to connect with her and enjoy her contributions more in the future!"

- A Director of Recruiting, Lincoln Financial Advisors

- Worked with Aderonke at Lincoln Financial Advisors

6. "Aderonke is an outstanding project manager. She has exceptional leadership skills and tremendous focus. Aderonke effectively manages project teams by focusing on day-to-day tasks as well as by having a forward-looking, big-picture view of short- and long-term goals required to achieve project success. Aderonke willingly goes the extra mile whenever necessary to ensure that projects are completed on time, on budget, and to the customer's satisfaction.

7. "Always professional, courteous, and friendly. Although I did not work on the same projects with her, Aderonke's strong work ethic was apparent. She is committed to excellence and raising the bar."

- A New Business Coordinator, Lincoln Financial Advisors

- Worked with Aderonke at Lincoln Financial Advisors

8. "Aderonke is a very articulate, intelligent person that uses her business skills not only to benefit her company but to also benefit the community that she is a part of. Ade is able to initiate projects quickly that are well-thought-out and then implement them on a timely basis. She is a great team player and supportive of those that she works with."

   • An Owner, Car Dealership

   • Was with another company when working with Aderonke at Lincoln Financial Advisors

9. "I worked with Aderonke for one year after she relocated to Salt Lake City as executive projects coordinator. She was fantastic to work with and exceeded expectations with every task assigned. Aderonke is never afraid to try something new and quickly builds relationships and finds a way to add value. If you would like more detail, I would be happy to reply or take your calls."

   • An Executive Director, Lincoln Financial Advisors

   • Managed Aderonke at Lincoln Financial Advisors

10. "Aderonke displayed exceptional professional and interpersonal qualities during our time as colleagues. She was extremely dedicated to her position and creating outstanding work product. She was very easy to work with and generally went beyond the scope of her duties to help others, which definitely makes a team player. She is a pleasure to have around in a professional environment."

- A Paralegal, Lincoln Financial Group

- Worked with Aderonke at Lincoln Financial Group

11. "Aderonke has a great understanding of web architecture and user experience. She was extremely helpful in managing our consumer website and keeping it relevant for site visitors. She's proactive, strategic, and resourceful. It is my pleasure to provide an endorsement."

- An AVP, Corporate Branding & Advertising, Lincoln Financial Group

- Managed Aderonke indirectly at Lincoln Financial Group

The satisfaction from these and others who I had worked with, including a CEO of a Fortune 500 company and other executive-level colleagues, remain priceless, repeatedly giving me joy and satisfaction from the projects that I had delivered.

BENEFITS FOR PROJECT MANAGERS

YES, IF WE have never met in person, you may just be asking why you should even listen to me. Yes, you see that it may be fun to work on a variety of projects. And it might be fulfilling to have so many recommendations, but what is beyond that? Why should anyone consider becoming a project manager? Here are a few more reasons:

1. **A Hidden Gem:** Project management is like a hidden gem that not enough people have discovered. At a time when many jobs are becoming obsolete to technology, there is no end in sight for the career of project management. There is lots of room for many more individuals in the career. There are always jobs available in the market.

- **Never Gets Boring:** I have served in this career for well over seventeen years and could probably do another seventeen years. I am still as happy and content as I have been ever day since I first started.

- **Work-from-Home Flexibility:** During the COVID-19 pandemic, many jobs allowed its people to work from home. This might be temporary for some. Most project managers are not required to work in an office. They can perform their work successfully from many different locations, even overseas sometimes.

- **Travel Flexibility:** Early in many corporate consulting careers, individuals get to travel to client sites, enjoy hotel luxuries, and store up airline miles. This usually becomes less as most people rise the ranks. For many project managers, they can find roles that best suit their preferences and allow them to travel as little or as much as they feel like throughout their careers.

- **Transfers:** It is not always easy to transfer from one field of work to the other, but for project managers, it is much easier. A project manager who has worked for several years in the legal field typically does not have a hard time transferring their skills into the finance, human resources, marketing, or technology fields as a project manager. The focus is always delivery, and the tenets that make a successful project manager are usually independent of one's field. The opportunities to easily transfer from one field within project management to another are many.

- **Fast Way Up:** Many in the workforce are typically striving to get to management and executive leadership. What many never verbalize is the fact that project management careers are a speedy way to get to the top. When executive positions open and the search team looks within their organization, they are typically looking for people with a track record of delivering well for the organization. Project managers usually soar to the top, and so you will see that many project managers quickly rise into poles like chief of staff, chief administrative officer and chief operating officer.

There are so many benefits to being a project manager; this list merely touches the tip.

LANDING YOUR FIRST OPPORTUNITY

AS I SAT back preparing to write this book, I thought about what would be important to those who were undecided about a career or aspiring to be project managers. I realized it would be important to show the way forward and therefore sought insight from other successful project managers on how they landed their first opportunity. For many project managers, entry into the field was atypical, but I hope some of these thoughts and recommendations from current project managers based are helpful as you chart your own path:

1. Start by getting a lot of project team member experience and then raise your hand when the right opportunity comes.

2. Put in the hours, showing leadership where you can. Work your way up. The whole profession to me is merit-based.

3. I took on as much extra small work as possible with anyone who wanted my help in the office and took a project manager as a mentor.

4. I started as a project coordinator intern, and I told them in my interview that I aspire to become a project manager. I've now been managing projects for the same company for the last six months.

5. I graduated from a MSc. And only then a company gave me the opportunity to start as a project manager.

6. I moved up the ladder as a team leader for a consulting firm, and I then got a PG diploma in project management. I joined as a project manager after that.

7. I started at the bottom at the IT company I work for and showed them I wanted more and more! I had a knack for coordination, and they thought I would be good as a project manager.

8. By accident, I was in sales, and when I was not meant for that, I was put into an IT project and grew from that.

9. I networked.

10. I landed my first role through a department transfer. I was already in the industry and proved that I was organized and analytical. Then I was asked to switch.

11. I think it is important to make your intentions known to your current employer/managers. Share how you can use

your knowledge in the project manager space, even if it does not directly correlate to your current role.

12. I honestly fell into project management. I lost my job in the mortgage industry. I then took an entry-level position at a pharmaceutical company and worked my way up. One thing led to another.

13. I went to a university for architecture, landed a job at a general contractor that built fast-food restaurants, and ended up with a project manager mentor. Eventually I moved on to another job in a different city with an opportunity to manage bigger projects on higher education campuses.

14. I was already manager of a large IT programming group after Y2K and asked to help establish a PMO.

15. I worked as an analyst in health care for a few years before I went in as a decision support advisor/analyst into a PMO/process improvement team in health care. I had project management courses as part of my master's degree. Then I got trained on the job and built networking within the organization. Then I was offered to switch roles from analytics to project manager.

16. I was doing more hands-on integration/QA work. Then I started doing more coordination work, which led to more managing teams and projects. It is easier when you can move around within a company.

17. I got promoted within. It was not my intention or direction. It was just a combination of hard work in other related areas (which I did not realize at the time) and being at the right place at the right time. I have been a project manager for five years now at my company, and I love it.

18. I got promoted from within. They saw the potential in me and paid for all the education and training.

19. It was recession time, and my boss noticed I could manage three projects at a time, so I stayed while others left. I taught myself to manage seven projects at a time. A recession is a bad time, but if you are prepared to manage while others are not, your value will be seen.

20. I volunteered for other projects as a coordinator first to build experience and visibility.

21. I started as an executive assistant at a small company and got roped into managing a system migration and grew from there. Four years are down now, and I hope to keep growing. I also landed my PMP certificate.

22. I jumped from service management to project management with help from my manager as he saw potential in me as I proved myself many times in small activities I can take a lead. Also I did all project-related training provided by company and whatever was available in the market at that point.

23. I spoke to anyone I knew in business, asking if they knew anyone who had any opportunities. I worked voluntarily for a while. The experience was worth tenfold. I used this experience to then get me through the interviews for a more serious role.

24. Someone took a chance on me.

25. Accidentally, however, I had the drive, passion, and common sense without the accreditation. The exams came second.

26. Mine was not a direct path. I did some rigorous transformational training for two years, which is great prep for project management. I volunteered my time to lead, manage, and develop teams by coaching leadership programs outside of work. I stepped up whenever the project manager was out in one of my previous jobs. (He was out frequently throughout the year for one to four weeks.)

27. One could say it happened by accident, but I also did a lot of internal work on myself and was very clear on what I was looking for.

In reading the various experiences, it was clear that there is not one direct path as with medical doctors or lawyers, but what I hope you might get from this is some inspiration and the confirmation that anyone can become a project manager regardless of your education, interests, or experience. You are welcome to contact me for specific advice, résumé reviews, interview preparations, and more guidance on landing your first opportunity.

LESSONS LEARNED AS A PROJECT MANAGER

OFTEN, WHEN PROJECT managers think of lessons learned, they are thinking of an activity that follows the completion of a project. This is different. Even before you embark on the journey of becoming a project manager, here are a few key but simple lessons I learned over the course of my career as a project manager:

1. Communication is key. Ensure all stakeholders are informed.

2. Set the direction. Proactively managing the process and your stakeholder reduces chaos.

3. Your stakeholders are human. Senior executives and lower-level staff are people just alike.

4. Do not start until you are ready. Great first impressions allow for later wins.

5. The messenger is not the message. Tools are just tools. The information is what matters.

6. You cannot do it all alone. If you treat people well, they will go to bat for you.

7. Give yourself a break. It is not rocket science or heart surgery. If something slips, it will work out.

8. Play games with correct strategy. The PMP test is a test of regurgitation and not necessarily actual experience. Do not make that mistake

9. PMP boot camps are worth it. What you will learn in a week could also take you forever.

10. Get certified. This certification opens doors. Get the PMP and maintain it.

11. You will meet knuckleheads. Ignore the silliness and stay above the fray.

12. Stay flexible. No two projects are different. The day you get rigid is the day you begin to fail.

13. Friendships are not required. Project owners just want their projects done on time and on budget.

14. Fix it and move on. Mistakes will happen, but you do not have time to waste.

15. You are the captain of your ship. Your project needs you. Do not lose sight of your significance.

16. Leverage your people. Investing in people and empowering them to shine as experts in their own field will make you look good.

17. Resilience is key. Some days may be hard, but hard days are usually short-lived.

18. Keep progressing. When you are not progressing, you are regressing even deeper.

19. Etch it in ink. People will forget what they told you.

20. Knowledge is power. Read research articles to stay abreast of the topic at hand.

21. Organization is key. Your level of organization determines the organization of the project

These suggestions are not only lessons learned but happen to be keys to being successful as a project manager.

ROUNDING IT UP

You have heard it all. You now understand what it means to be a project manager, what types of projects you can get involved with, the benefits, the secrets to success, and so much more. Although this book is not exhaustive, I hope it at least gives you some perspective on why you should seriously consider this career.

If it at least sparked your interest further, please let my team know by writing a review or emailing info@becomingapm.com. In addition, if you need additional help, we would be glad to support you at www.becomingapm.com.

We cannot wait to see more converts and write more books that will help you be successful in your career as a project manager.

REFERENCES

Dictionary, O. E. 1989. Oxford English Dictionary. Simpson, JA & Weiner, ESC.

Merry, P. 2000. *Project Management T-Kit*.

Dixon, M. (ed.). 2000. *Body of Knowledge: Project Management*. Association for Project Management.

Fayol, H. 1916. "General Principles of Management." *Classics of Organization Theory* 2(15): 57–69.

Jones, N. L. 2013. *Chapter Two: Of Poetry and Politics: The Managerial Culture of Sixteenth-Century England*. Kaufman, Peter Iver.

Malik, F. 2015. *Managing Performing Living: Effective Management for a New World*. Campus Verlag.

Guide, P. M. B. O. K. 2004. "A Guide to the Project Management Body of Knowledge." In *Project Management Institute* (vol. 3).

ABOUT THE AUTHOR

Dr. Addie Adelekan is a consulting project manager who served as chief operating officer of AVF Consulting and as director of technology at Jitasa Group. In addition to managing projects, she spends a significant amount of time in philanthropy. She received her undergraduate degree in information systems from Howard University in Washington, D.C., an MBA from Washington University in St. Louis, and a Ph.D. in organizational leadership from Regent University in Virginia. She lives in Washington, D.C. with her two children. She is also the author of *Raising Good Leaders: A Guide for Parents and Educators.*

www.ingramcontent.com/pod-product-compliance
Lightning Source LLC
Chambersburg PA
CBHW031502210526
45463CB00003B/1031